HILLSBORO PUBLIC LIBRARY
HILLSBORO, OR 97124
MEMBER OF WASHINGTON COUNTY
COOPERATIVE LIBRARY SERVICES

FIRST SCIENCE

Electricity

by Mari Schuh

Consultant:
Duane Quam, M.S. Physics
Chair, Minnesota State Academic

HILLSBORO PUBLIC LIBRARY
HILLSBORO, OR 97124
MEMBER OF WASHINGTON COUNTY
COOPERATIVE LIBRARY SERVICES

BLASTOFF! 4 READERS

BELLWETHER MEDIA • MINNEAPOLIS, MN

Note to Librarians, Teachers, and Parents:

Blastoff! Readers are carefully developed by literacy experts and combine standards-based content with developmentally-appropriate text.

Level 1 provides the most support through repetition of high-frequency words, light text, predictable sentence patterns, and strong visual support.

Level 2 offers early readers a bit more challenge through varied simple sentences, increased text load, and less repetition of high frequency words.

Level 3 advances early-fluent readers toward fluency through increased text and concept load, less reliance on visuals, longer sentences, and more literary language.

Level 4 builds reading stamina by providing more text per page, increased use of punctuation, greater variation in sentence patterns, and increasingly challenging vocabulary.

Level 5 encourages children to move from "learning to read" to "reading to learn" by providing even more text, varied writing styles, and less familiar topics.

Whichever book is right for your reader, Blastoff! Readers are the perfect books to build confidence and encourage a love of reading that will last a lifetime!

This edition first published in 2008 by Bellwether Media.

No part of this publication may be reproduced in whole or in part without written permission of the publisher. For information regarding permission, write to Bellwether Media Inc., Attention: Permissions Department, Post Office Box 1C, Minnetonka, MN 55345-9998.

Library of Congress Cataloging-in-Publication Data
Schuh, Mari C., 1975–
    Electricity / by Mari Schuh.
        p. cm. – (Blastoff! readers) (First science)
Summary: "First Science explains introductory physical science concepts about electricity through real-world observation and simple scientific diagrams. Intended for students in grades three through six"—Provided by publisher.
    Includes bibliographical references and index.
    ISBN-13: 978-1-60014-095-2 (hardcover : alk. paper)
    ISBN-10: 1-60014-095-5 (hardcover : alk. paper)   37577250   5/08
    1. Electricity–Juvenile literature. I. Title.

QC527.2.S39 2008
537–dc22   2007010296

Text copyright © 2008 by Bellwether Media.
SCHOLASTIC, CHILDREN'S PRESS, and associated logos are trademarks and/or registered trademarks of Scholastic Inc. Printed in the United States of America.

Contents

What Is Electricity?

Have you used electricity today? Electricity runs your clock. It toasts your bread and keeps the food in your refrigerator cold.

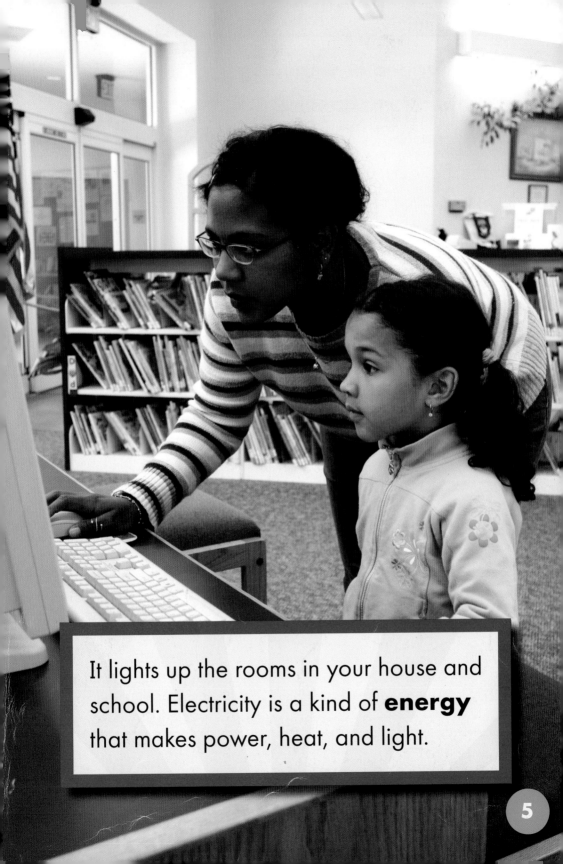

It lights up the rooms in your house and school. Electricity is a kind of **energy** that makes power, heat, and light.

Electricity begins with **atoms**. Atoms are tiny building blocks that make up everything in the world. They are so small that millions of them would fit on the tip of your pencil! Atoms have even smaller parts inside them called **electrons**. Electrons can move very fast from one atom to another. Moving electrons create electricity.

fun fact

An electric eel is a fish that makes electricity from chemicals inside its body. It shocks other fish in order to catch and eat them.

atom

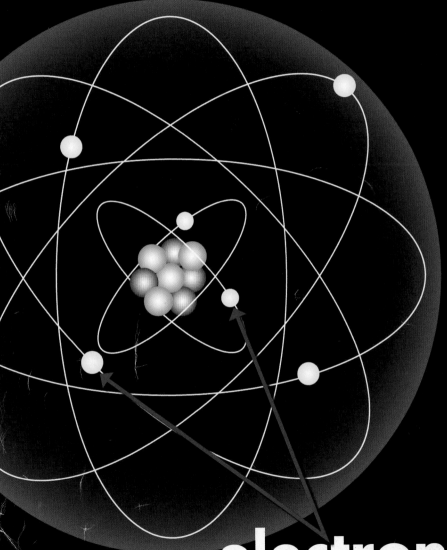

electron

Electric Currents

Most of the time moving electrons flow along a path, like water in a river. This is called an electric **current**. An electric current moves through metal wires inside the walls of your house. These wires carry electricity to **outlets** or **switches**. Flip a switch. You're using electricity!

fun fact

Electricity is even in your body! Nerves carry electric charges to and from your brain. These charges act like messages, telling your body how to work. They tell your arms to move and your lungs to breathe. The electric charges even tell your heart when to beat!

power lines

The electric current comes to your house through power lines high in the air or under the ground.

Those power lines start at big power plants. Power plants can make enough electricity for hundreds of houses or even an entire city.

11

The power lines from the power plants connect to wires in your home. Those wires connect to outlets or switches in your walls. The outlets provide power to lights and machines.

Electric wires usually have rubber or plastic around them. Electricity doesn't flow through rubber or plastic. Those materials keep the electricity inside the wire.

Batteries

Batteries can also make electricity. Watches, cameras, flashlights, and many toys all get their electricity from batteries. Batteries use energy from **chemicals** inside them to create an electric current. Batteries let you take electricity anywhere.

15

Static Electricity

Static electricity is a kind of electricity that doesn't move in a current. Static electricity comes from two objects rubbing together. Electrons rub off of one object and stick to the other, giving both an **electric charge**.

This makes the two objects either stick together or push apart. Static electricity can make the hairs on your head push apart from each other.

A flash of light brightens the night sky. It's lightning! Did you know that lightning is caused by static electricity? That's right. When ice crystals in a cloud rub together, they create electricity. The electricity can build up in the cloud. Lightning is electricity moving from one cloud to another cloud or to the ground.

! fun fact

The telephone is a machine that turns the sounds of your voice into an electric current that can be sent to another phone. The other phone turns the electric current back into the sounds of your voice.

Be Safe Around Electricity

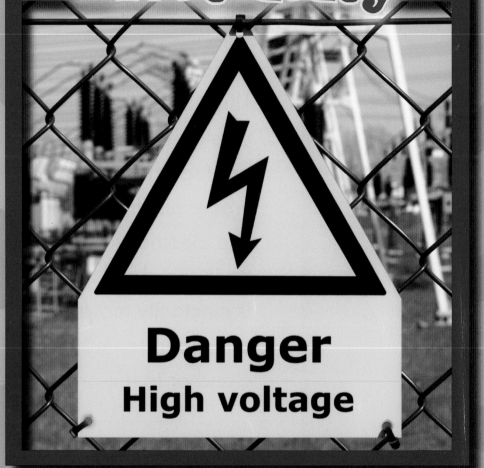

Danger

High voltage

Electricity helps people in many ways. It could also hurt you if you touch it. Be very careful with electricity. Never play with cords or outlets. Go inside your house if you see lightning.

Electricity powers computers and televisions. It helps you see after dark. It makes life easier and more fun. What would life be like without electricity?

Glossary

atom—very tiny particles; atoms are the building blocks for everything in the world.

batteries—containers with chemicals inside them; batteries turn chemical energy into electricity.

chemical—a substance used in a chemical process

current—the flow of electrons through a wire or other material

electric charge—the amount of electricity in an object

electron—a small part inside an atom; electrons carry an electric charge; electrons moving from atom to atom make electricity.

energy—the ability to do work

outlet—a small area, often on a wall, where objects can be plugged in to get electricity

static electricity—electricity made by rubbing two objects together

switch—a device, such as a light switch, used to open or close an electric circuit

To Learn More

AT THE LIBRARY

Bailey, Jacqui. *Charged Up: The Story of Electricity*. Minneapolis, Minn.: Picture Window Books, 2004.

Stille, Darlene R. *Electricity*. Chanhassen, Minn.: Child's World, 2005.

Trumbauer, Lisa. *What Is Electricity*. New York: Children's Press, 2003.

ON THE WEB

Learning more about electricity is as easy as 1, 2, 3.

1. Go to www.factsurfer.com

2. Enter "electricity" into search box.

3. Click the "Surf" button and you will see a list of related web sites.

With factsurfer.com, finding more information is just a click away.

Index

The images in this book are reproduced through the courtesy of: Tyler Boyes, front cover; Andrew Crawford/Getty Images, p. 4; marmion, p. 5; Linda Clavel, pp. 6-7; Boden/Ledingham/Masterfile, p. 8; Joellen L. Armstrong, p. 9; Petra Silhava, pp. 10-11; Dimitri Sherman, p. 12; Mariano N. Ruiz, p. 13; Adam Marjchrzak, pp. 14-15; Phil Degginger/Alamy, p. 16; Anthony Redpath, p. 17; Ralph H. Wetmore II/Getty Images, pp. 18-19; Katharina Wittfeld, p. 20; Jeffrey Schmieg, p. 21.